T0149834

CHINESE
TEA

Discovering China

CHINESE
TEA

LING YUN

Better Link Press

This book is edited and designed by the Editorial Committee of *Cultural China* series

Managing Directors: Wang Youbu, Xu Naiqing
Editorial Director: Wu Ying
Editor: Anna Nguyen

Text and photographs: Ling Yun

Interior and Cover Design: Wang Wei
Cover Image: Quanjing

ISBN: 978-1-60220-106-4

Address any comments about *Discovering China: Chinese Tea* to:

Better Link Press
99 Park Ave
New York, NY 10016
USA

or

Shanghai Press and Publishing Development Company, Ltd.
F 7 Donghu Road, Shanghai, China (200031)
Email: comments_betterlinkpress@hotmail.com

Printed in China by Shenzhen Donnelley Printing Co., Ltd.

3   4   5   6   7   8   9   10

CONTENTS

Tea culture is an integral part of life for the Chinese people.

FOREWORD

The Chinese regarded tea as a daily necessity along with the essential seasonings of their vibrant cuisine. Lin Yutang, a famous writer once commented, "With a teapot, a Chinese is happy wherever he/she goes." On the other hand, the well-educated and sophisticated ancient Chinese considered "lute-playing, chess, calligraphy, painting, poem, opera and tea art" as the seven landmark artistic skills that they must acquire. The core of Oriental culture is demonstrated in the process of tea-making, from the boiling to the drinking ceremony, as well as the delicate philosophy behind it.

You might be pleasantly surprised by how much better you'll feel by drinking tea. Let's explore its Zen-like qualities of calmness and harmony and the stories behind it.

唐竟陵陸羽鴻漸撰

一之源

茶者南方之嘉木也一尺二尺迺至數十尺其
巴山峽川有兩人合抱者伐而掇之其樹如瓜
蘆葉如梔子花如白薔薇實如栟櫚葉如丁香
根如胡桃瓜蘆木出廣州似茶至苦澀栟櫚蒲葵之屬其子似茶胡桃與茶根皆下
孕兆至瓞礫苗木上抽其字或從草或從木或從草木并_{從草}
當作茶其字出開元文字者義從木當作搽其字出本草草木并作茶其字出爾雅其名

The Classic of Tea written by Lu Yu

8

CHAPTER ONE

HISTORY AND CUSTOMS

After its discovery, tea was restricted to the corner of Southwest China due to the inconvenience of transportation for about 2,400 years.

It was not until 316 BC when the great-great-grandfather of the First Emperor Qin Shihuang, King Hui of Qin Kingdom, conquered the small Kingdom of Shu in Sichuan Province that tea was enjoyed by the power elite class. His troops brought tea back to his kingdom in the central area of China, which caused

Terracotta warriers, discovered in Qin Shihuang's mausoleum, display the strenght of might of the Qin army, whose forefathers brought tea to the central area of China in 316 BC.

A lady from the Tang dynasty invented the tea bowl with saucer to avoid the hot water from scalding her.

its popularity to grow among the masses.

In the Tang dynasty, tea culture was brought into full blossom with its strong national power, prolific creativity and extensive tolerance for great diversity.

During this period, Lu Yu (733-804 AD) also emerged as a ground-breaking figure in the history of the Chinese tea culture. The author of *The Classic of Tea*, later generations honored him as "the Sage of Tea." And tea was established as a "national drink" since then.

A lady from the Tang dynasty invented the tea bowl with saucer to avoid the hot water from scalding her. This kind of tea set was popular in the following dynasties, which has now become the *gaiwan* (cup bowl with saucer and lid).

In a painting from the Tang dynasty,

Revelry in Tang Court from the Tang dynasty

Rabbit's hair-patterned cup from the Song dynasty, Jian Kiln

Chaxian (the tea whisk). The leaves were ground to fine powder in a small stone mill, and the preparation was whipped in hot water by a delicate whisk made of split bamboo.

we can see 12 noble ladies drinking tea together. There is a big vessel for holding tea on the center of a large bamboo-surface table. A lady is pouring tea for the others. We can see that people at that time were still using big porcelain bowls instead of cups to drink tea. The ladies are gathered in a relaxed atmosphere, showing their back or front, standing or sitting. They're playing different traditional Chinese musical instruments like a folk music quartet, with a maid playing castanet at one side to match the rhythm, holding a silk fan, listening to music with a bowl in hand, or simply enjoying the tea in graceful manner. In addition, a pup silently rests under the table…

Tea art reached another peak during the Song dynasty. Zhao Ji, Emperor

Painting of *A Decent Party* drawn by Emperor Huizong from the Song dynasty

A bird's view of the Forbidden City

Huizong of the Song dynasty, was more a gifted artist than an emperor. As an expert in calligraphy, painting and musical instruments, Zhao Ji also had an inexhaustible zest for tea. He was adept in all the popular arts of tea of his time, and had an eye for fine tea utensils. For a better appreciation of the foam from white tea, he highly recommended the black rabbit's hair-patterned cup.

Emperor Huizong is known as the only one among past emperors, that wrote a book about tea. The book, *General Remarks on Tea*, condensed in less than three thousand words, fully elaborates his ingenious ideas on tea. Equally important in the Song dynasty was a highly skillful form of tea art called "various tea games". Emperor Huizong was said to have learned it and even performed it in front of the court officials.

The founder of the Ming dynasty, Zhu Yuanzhang (1328-1398), issued a decree to start the use of loose tea, the same tea form as we see today. And the tea sets were largely reduced to a few minimum as compared with the

The tea house in the Qing dynasty

original "24 utensils." This reform of tea-drinking six hundred years ago generally led to the modern form of tea-drinking in China.

The form of tea-drinking in the Ming dynasty was followed in the Qing dynasty. As the most longest-living Chinese emperor, Qianlong (1711-1799) believed that the key to his regimen was tea. Four of his six inspection trips to the south, he visited the hometown of "Xihu Longjing." Nowadays, you may see that the Chinese often give a light knock at the tea table or dining table to thank the one serving the tea. This custom originated from Qianlong.

The form of the Song kettle

A thank-you knock

17

Process of producing Longjing tea

CHAPTER TWO

10 MOST POPULAR CHINESE TEAS

As an old saying goes, "Tea names are too many to remember, even for a life-long tea drinker." China has the largest variety of teas among all countries with over hundreds of superb kinds with worldly fame. What are the top 10? I believe the answer is subjective like *People* magazine's 50 "Most Beautiful People."

Through several thousand years, the varieties and processing methods of Chinese tea have undergone tremendous change from one dynasty to another. The use of some splendid ancient teas declines or even becomes extinct as new teas emerge in every era. Each new tea excels the last one, similar to how the waves that are behind in the Yang-

Modern Chinese Tea	Categories	Features	Typical Types	Remarks
Six Tea Categories	Green Tea	Non-fermented	*①Xihu Longjing、 *②Bi Luo Chun、 *③Huangshan Maofeng、 Pingshui Zhucha (pearl-shaped tea)、 Taipin Houkui、 Lushan Yunwu、 Tunlu、 Guzhu Zisun (Purple Bamboo Shoot)、 Xinyang Maojian	Chinese green teas have the richest choices.
	Black Tea	Fully Fermented	*④Qimen Black Tea (Keemun)、 Yunnan Black Tea 、 Zhengshan Xiaozhong	
	Yellow Tea	Stacked	*⑤Junshan Yinzhen、 Mengding Huangya (Yellow Bud)	
	White Tea	Steamed	*⑥Baihao Yinzhen、 White Peony、 Shoumei	
	Oolong Tea	Semi-fermented	*⑦Anxi Tie Guan Yin (Tieh Kwan Yin)、 Huang Jingui	Grow in South Fujian
			*⑧Da Hong Pao (Red Robe)、 TieLuohan、 Bai Jiguan、 Shui Jingui、 Shuixian、 Rougui	Grow in North Fujian
			*⑪Fenghuang Dancong	Grow in Guangdong
			*⑫Baihao Oolong、 Dongding Oolong	Grow in Taiwan
	Dark Tea	Compressed	*⑨Pu'er Tea	Special definition
			Other Tea Bricks and Bowl Tea	
Reprocessing Tea	Scented Tea	Flower-scented	*⑩Jasmine Tea、 Rose Tea	Scented
			*Red Point、 Seven Fairladies	Artistic tea

* Highlighted in future chapter Major Tea Categories

tze River drive on those in front. Every variety of tea has its own rise and fall in history.

First, we should know that the same fresh green leaves, as raw material, will turn into totally different processed tea. Modern tea can be divided into six major categories due to the diverse processing methods, as in the following chart. The 7th category is scented tea. It is a unique variety of tea, which doesn't belong to any of the six major tea categories. It has a reprocessing process, during which, ready-made green tea, black tea, Oolong of the six major teas will be blended with fresh flowers. The tea leaves will slowly absorb the scent of the flowers in stillness. After a while, the farmers screen out the flower residue and dry the leaves, and the scented tea will be obtained.

Green Tea: The majority of the famous teas in China are green teas. They contain more nutrients and chlorophyll compared with other teas due to the absence of fermentation during processing. Based on the production method, green teas include the fired ones such as Longjing and Bi Luo Chun, and steamed ones were popular in China before Ming dynasty, nowadays there is Yulu of Japan that have a fresh jade-green color.

Yellow Tea: The production is similar to that of green tea, however, it is stacked so that its liquor appears yellow. Famous kinds are Junshan Yinzhen and Mengding Yellow Bud.

White Tea: It is steamed to retain its taste and scent of sunshine. Typical types are Baihao Yinzhen, Shoumei, and White Peony.

Oolong Tea: This unique Chinese tea variety, also known as semi-fermented, possesses distinctive characteristics, featured by both the fermentation of black tea and non-fermentation of green tea. The tea leaves are red at edge and green in the center after brewing. The varieties of Oolong include Tie Guan Yin tea, Wuyi rock tea and Taiwan Oolong.

Black Tea: This type is actually called red tea in Chinese. Full-fermention causes the red liquor in the cup.

The popular ones are Qimen black tea, Yunnan black tea and Zhengshan Xiaozhong.

Dark Tea: These leaves are compressed into shapes of bricks, cakes, and bowls, for long-distance transportation and storage. Some teas in this category are Pu'er Tea, Liubao tea and Hunan dark tea.

The portrait of Emperor Qianlong

Now, let's learn more about some of the most popular Chinese teas today. They are the representatives of the 6 tea types mentioned above, most of which have unarguably led the list of the Top 10 teas for a very long time. Available at Chinese tea shops, these teas, full of pride and joy, wait for tea lovers to bring them home to enjoy.

The map of Longjing Tea Area from the Qing dynasty

Xihu Longjing

Xihu Longjing tea has long been in first place among the Chinese teas. The tea gets its name, Longjing which means Dragon Well in Chinese, from the saying that a dragon once drank from a well there.

Crowned as "the queen of green tea," she was born in Hangzhou City, Zhejiang Province in East China. This city, called "heaven on earth," gets its fame from its beautiful West Lake (Xihu). The area producing Xihu Longjing tea is not far from West Lake. It is surrounded by mountains on three sides, which forms a natural barrier for a unique microclimate. Historically, five spots in this area produced the best Xihu Longjing tea. Now the finest ones are mainly from three spots, Shifeng Mountain, Meijia Wu and Xihu Longjing Village. Among the three, Shifeng (Lion Mount) Xihu Longjing is considered the highest quality.

Longjing tea is famous for its jade-green color, delicate aroma, mellow taste and beauty of shape. Its appearance is characterized by smoothness, flatness, and straightness. Longjing tea is best when the leaves are fresh.

Have you heard of the term called "*Mingqian* Tea"? It means that farmers pick the tea before the Qingming Festival, which takes place in the 5th solar term of April. Known for its superior quality, *Mingqian* tea has tender buds and a rich fragrant smell. Unfortunately, *Mingqian* tea is especially rare. This means pre-Qingming Xihu Longjing tea is as expensive as fresh seafood such as fine Australian lobster or South African oysters, with the price changing everyday! *Mingqian* Shifeng Longjing's color isn't a common green like many would expect. The leaves contain some natural

West Lake (Xihu)

Xihu Longjing

Suzhou garden in spring

yellowish notes like that of brown rice.

Bi Luo Chun (Pi Lo Chun)

This tea is produced in Dongting Mountain in Wu County of Suzhou City, Jiangsu Province of East China. Another heavenly place like Hangzhou, Suzhou is the place where Xi Shi (during Spring and Autumn period), one of the most beautiful ladies in Chinese history, often spent her holidays 2500 years ago. Tea gardens and orchards grow here in the neighborhoods, bringing a special floral aroma and fruity taste to Bi Luo Chun.

Both considered supreme green teas, Bi Luo Chun and Xihu Longjing tea are easy to distinguish from each other be-

Incised windows of East China and Bi Luo Chun tea both feature delicacy. Collection of Guanfu Classic Art Museum.

Bi Luo Chun

Huangshan Mountain

cause of their different processing techniques. Xihu Longjing is pressed flat, while Bi Luo Chun is rolled into a tight spiral and has a dark green color with snowy white hairs.

The most precious Bi Luo Chun tea is the pre-Qingming, cropped and processed from Spring Equinox to Qingming Festival.

Huangshan Maofeng

Huangshan Maofeng, the most well-known Alpine green tea in China, originates from Anhui Province. It grows in the highest mountain in the eastern part of the country unlike Xihu Longjing and Bi Luo Chun. Huangshan Mountain is deemed the most famous Chinese

Huangshan Maofeng

mountain for its four wonders: strange-ly-shaped pines, grotesque rock forma-tions, seas of clouds and hot springs. The environment is suited for the growth of tea with its high elevation, fine soil tex-ture, and a warm and humid climate. It is "foggy everywhere from morning until night on a fine day, while cloudy when it's gloomy or rainy."

Top class Huangshan Maofeng has looks like gold pieces with ivory hair. The tea soap appears clear, and the light yel-low tea leaves look like flowers in it.

Qimen Black Tea (Keemun or Qi-hong)

While it appears that black tea comes from red leaves, the full fermenta-

A typical tea shop of Huizhou of the Qing dynasty

The Huizhou houses

Fine black tea

Qimen black tea

tion process causes the green leaves to turn a dark color.

Qimen black tea comes from the southwestern part of Anhui Province, near the production area of Huang-shan Maofeng. The area that grows Qimen black tea has an advantageous natural condition: a great number of woods in a mountainous region, a warm and humid climate, and thick layers of earth with abundant rainfall, and cloudy or foggy weather most days of the year. The rich contents and high enzymatic activity in the soil make the local tea trees suitable for creating black tea. During the first year in the reign of Emperor Guangxu (in the year 1875), an Anhuinese resident and merchant, who admired the popularity of Fujian black tea, made the first successful batch of Qimen black tea.

The Chinese began drinking black tea in the Southern Song dynasty over one thousand years ago. The Chinese prefer to drink black tea plain while the British prefer to drink it with milk and sugar along with some cakes as breakfast tea or afternoon tea. Black tea shines even more brilliantly in the company of Wedgwood or Royal Albert drinkware. The tea's taste remains strong after milk is added. Thereafter, two styles of drinking black tea are formed. We can say that black tea originated in China, and further developed in Britain into the practice of afternoon tea.

Anxi Tie Guan Yin (Tieh Kwan Yin)

Tie Guan Yin, the most typical Oolong tea, grows in Anxi County in the south of Fujian Province. The tea trees are planted in curved lines on the southeast slope of the mountain. From the sky, it looks like a carefully designed

Guan Yin (Kwan-yin) is the Goddess of Mercy. Her female image in China is featured by kindness and clemency. For this reason, she is highly valued by the Chinese Buddhists in China and common people often pray to her for good luck.

Anxi Tie Guan Yin

green labyrinth. During the late Qing dynasty, Anxi Tie Guan Yin (Tieh Kwan Yin) was successively introduced to Taiwan Province and Guangdong Province, which promoted the development of Oolong tea there.

How do you recognize Tie Guan Yin from other teas? Granular Tie Guan Yin weighs more than others in the same volume. It's rolled in balls before steeped in water. When fully infused, green tea leaves with red rims can clearly be seen. It differs from other Oolong teas for its natural orchid aroma and special appeal called "Guan Yin Yun" (mainly referring to its strong perfume, bursting flavor and lingering aftertaste).

Da Hong Pao (Scarlet Robe or Red Robe)

Wuyi rock tea, a famous kind of Oolong in China, grows on the Wuyi Mountain of Fujian Province. The tea Da Hong Pao (Red Robe) is outstanding among the rock teas. The tea trees come from Tianxin Yan Rock, but large tea gardens are not to be found here. There are only four tea trees growing at a sunken spot on the cliff called "Jiu-long Ke" (literally meaning "Nine Dragon Cave"). In the sunshine, the tea shoots glistens with a lovely lustre of reddish purple.

Despite its black and loose look, Da Hong Pao (Red Robe) actually has great brewing durability. Even after seven or eight infusions to keep the tea hot, its floral fragrance can still remain as if it penetrated the cover of the cup in an undispersed "cluster." The Da Hong Pao leaves can keep the "cluster" of aroma for a fairly long time at the bottom of the cup, which is called "bottom fragrance" or "cold fragrance" by tea masters.

Wuyi Mountain

Nowadays, tea farmers in Mount Wuyi will set up high aerial ladders instead of using monkeys. The total output of rock tea is limited because they can normally only pick about 11 *liang* (a unit of weight equal to 50 grams), The tea can now be produced and put into the market in batches with clone technology.

Da Hong Pao

Junshan Yinzhen (Jun Mountain Silver Needle)

Junshan Yinzhen is produced in Junshan Island at the center of Dongting Lake in Hunan Province, the second largest fresh water lake of China.

Junshan Yinzhen is a yellow tea that resembles the shape of a needle. Mainly composed by bud teas, it is called "gold

Dongting Lake

inlaid with jade" for its plump yet compact look with a golden shine and tiny white hairs. More attention has been paid to its appreciation value than other teas. It is a feast for the eyes to watch the infusion of Junshan Yinzhen through a transparent glass. In the hot water, the tea buds stand upright like silver needles, then sink gradually to the bottom, and rise up again slowly like the dancing concubines of Emperor Shun. This process repeats itself for three rises and falls. This is one of the most prominent features of Junshan Yinzhen.

Junshan Yinzhen

Baihao Yinzhen (White Hair Silver Needle)

Baihao Yinzhen, the supreme variety of white tea, comes from Fujian Province, a place known for producing the imperial tribute tea during the Song dynasty.

Baihao Yinzhen is made from single fresh buds, approximately 3 cm long, from newborn tea trees in the spring. Covered all over with white hairs, its color is neither verdant like green tea, crimson as black tea, nor as brown as Oolong tea. It is called "silver needle" for its lustre of silver green.

Pu'er Tea

"Cropped by grandfather, enjoyed by grandson," the process of Pu'er tea

Baihao Yinzhen

Shangri-La is the important town on the ancient "Tea-Horse Road" to Tibet. This route played a historical role in the solidarity and trades between the Han and Tibetan.

takes several decades from its harvest to drinking.

Pu'er, a kind of dark tea, comes from Yunnan Province where there are many subtropical forests. Different from other tea leaves, Pu'er tea is made from big-leaf tea tree in various shapes of "cakes." It is a type of dark tea which mainly uses coarse and old raw materials. Its tea soup distinguishes itself from other teas from its red wine-like look, soft and smooth taste as well as an aged aroma unique to itself.

In conclusion, Pu'er tea's quality improves the longer it's preserved, because of its purer taste. It is the only tea that is valued by its age. Some aged Pu'er tea in the tea stock of the Forbidden City has existed for a hundred years. It has

Pu'er tea

now become a hot spot for collection and investment as a "drinkable antique."

Scented Tea (Flower-scented Tea)

Scented tea is mainly from Fujian, Zhejiang, Anhui and Jiangsu Province, because these places also produce fresh flowers. Scented tea is named after the flowers used in its production. Some popular varieties include, jasmine tea, rose tea and osmanthus tea.

Scented tea is a unique variety of tea, which doesn't belong to any of the six major tea categories. It is made through a reprocessing process where ready-made teas from the six major teas are blended with fresh flowers. The tea leaves are left for a while to slowly absorb the scent of the flowers. The final step in the process involves the farmers screening out the flower residue and drying the leaves.

Being Beijing-born, I know quite well that scented tea, also called *xiang pian* (silvers of perfume), is extremely

Rose tea

Various flowers for scenting teas

popular in Northern China. A method of blending valuable perfume into supreme green tea already existed as early as 1000 years ago in the Song dynasty. One typical flower used to scent tea is jasmine. Chinese people love jasmine so much that there is a famous folk song about it. The melody was adopted by Puccini in his opera *Turandot*.

You can see an example of scented tea in the recent film *Marie Antoinette* directed by Sofia Coppola. When the French Queen played by Kirsten Dunst, invites her brother to look at a mysterious treasure from faraway Orient. She says, "The Emperor of China sent me this tea. Watch the flower (water pouring...). Isn't it divine?" While the two stare at the cup , a white fog rises from the exquisite china cup and they are surprised to see a red flower blossom slowly from a bunch of green tea. The queen proudly tells her brother that it's jasmine tea. This magic tea used by Marie Antoinette to show off her luxurious royal life is actually a kind of Chinese artistic tea. It hides the flowers in a tea ball bound by green tea leaves and expands when infused with boiling water.

Sofia Coppla let Marie Antoinette (by Kirsten Dunst) show Chinese artistic tea in the film.

There are corresponding atensils for each particular tea types.

CHAPTER THREE

TEA SETS

Even with a fine tea in hand, the right choice of tea utensils is still crucial for making a nice cup of tea. An ancient saying goes "The utensil is the father of tea," and the correct use of it will reveal not only its scientific function, but also the aesthetic appreciation of the drinker. First of all, you would not use a red wine glass to appreciate the bubbles called the "splendid stars of champagne." Secondly, the choice of the wide-brimmed champagne saucer or tall, thin champagne tulip depends on the occasion, visual effect or just drinker's personal preference. If you can understand this, then you will understand the requirements on choosing Chinese teawares.

Why is the knowledge of tea utensils more complex than that of wine glasses? Using the wrong utensils can result in wasting the precious tea. For instance, someone who uses glass cup and warm water to brew Tie Guan Yin could find the tea "tasteless with a lot of stalks and old leaves." Similarly, Longjing tea can taste bitter and astringent if infused with boiling water in a large porcelain kettle, and covered it for a long time before pouring it out. We will miss the joy in tea drinking if we make such mistakes.

Generally, we need to consider three factors when choosing tea utensils: the location, the number of drinkers, and the species of tea leaves. There are corresponding utensils for each particular tea types. For example, a superb green tea should be matched with colorless transparent glass without any ornamentation. Oolong tea should be steeped in refined *Zisha* (purple clay) teapots, scented tea in bowls with a cover to retain its aroma, and ordinary green tea in large porcelain teapots.

1. The ABCs of Tea Sets

3. *Gaiwan*–China's classic tea set. The claim that *gaiwan* is used informally with friends is wrong. In fact, I found that *gaiwan* was served even in royal banquets.

1-2. Boiling kettle with a stove

4. (Left) Cup for sniffing scent (Right) Little tea cup

5. Tea pot

6. Tea bowl (with a high-heel saucer)

7. Small dish for appreciating dry tea

8. Tea caddy

9-10. Fair mug with the filter

11. Duplex layer basin

12. Tea tray

14. Knife to divide the cake or brick tea

15. Tea towel

13. Teaspoon combination

16. Basin

17. A *Zisha*-made frog
toy with a cleaning brush

2. Features of *Zisha* Teapots

A Chinese tea addict usually holds a small teapot in hand for both infusing and drinking alone. It is known as the Yixing *Zisha* teapot, which appeared in the early Northern Song dynasty, and gained momentum in the Ming dynasty. "The clay in the teapot is worth even more than gold," according to a local saying.

Zisha teapots are very popular despite their high prices due to their advantages for tea drinkers.

Zisha pots can maintain freshness of the tea for long periods of time. They can also help bring out the tea's flavor. And the teapot has great artistry along with its ability to improve the taste of tea.

Lastly, these teapots command a high price due to the rarity of its raw material. In the whole world, *Zisha* clay (purple clay) is said to only exist in the Yellow Dragon Cave of Dingshan town in Yixing. It only takes up 3 percent of the entire clay there. Some have even made a for-

Zisha tea set

tune by simply buying up the market of *Zisha* clay.

How can I find a good *Zisha* teapot?

i. In an overview, the spout, mouth and handle of the teapot should all touch the surface of the table if turned upside down.

ii. The water pours out smoothly without leaks. When the tea is served, the water at the mouth of the teapot should immediately fall back to the belly, without dripping out of the mouth of the tea pot.

iii. Fill up the teapot with water and cover it with the lid.

Block up the pot mouth and turn

Yixin Cabinet-style *Zisha* Teapot after Qing dynasty

i.

ii.

iii.

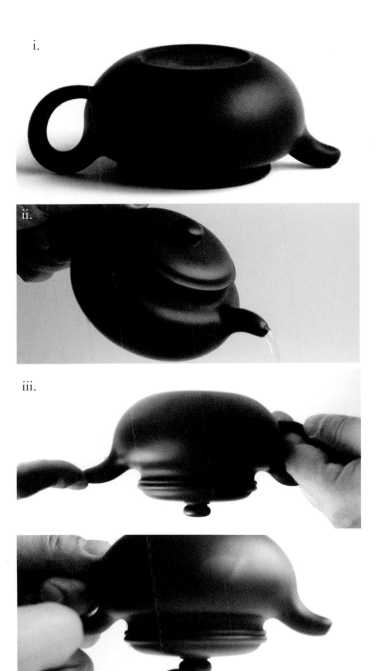

the pot upside down. It's a good pot if the lid doesn't fall,

Then keep the pot upside down, hold the lid while unblocking the mouth. It's also a sign of a good pot if the water doesn't come out.

Now that we've picked up a fine teapot, we need to be careful in its maintenance:

i. After you buy a teapot,cleanse it with water before boiling it in a large kettle of strong tea. After it cools off, boil it again. Repeat the whole process for three times, pick it up and dry it by airing. The teapot is now usable for tea making.

ii. When making tea, pour hot water in the pot and around it for several rounds, and then wipe the body of the teapot with wet towel or clean wet cloth for a while.

iii. After the temperature of the pot body goes down, you can also rub it with your own hands. The oil and sweat from your hands can help keep the pot body shiny and

i.

ii.

iii.

smooth. Keep doing it for three or four months, the teapot will have a better appearance.

Avoid getting greasy stains from food on the teapot.

3. Features of Porcelain Tea Utensils

Between the two major types of Chinese tea utensils, *Zisha* and ceramics, porcelain sets came much earlier and have been a part of the entire historical evolution of the Chinese tea.

Why are the porcelain tea utensils so dazzlingly distinct from the Tang, the Song and the Ming dynasties?

The reason is that the methods of tea drinking were different from one dynasty to the next. From brewing cake tea in the Tang dynasty, infusing powdered tea in the Song dynasty, to steeping leaf tea in the Ming dynasty, many ancient Chinese tea drinkers cared about not only the shape of the utensils in releasing the best taste of the tea soup, but also matching the color of the tea to evoke the high-

The clay-made cooker with caddy and pot in it (Original porcelain, Han dynasty)

A blue glazed porcelain tea bowl with a saucer (Southern dynasties)

Rabbit's hair-patterned cup from the Song dynasty, Jian Kiln

A tea bowl and saucer of Jun Kiln (Song dynasty)

est sense of aesthetic beauty. The special interest of ancient Oriental people in tea sets reflected their pursuit of a high quality life.

The first mature form of blue glazed porcelain emerged in the Shangyu district of Zhejiang Province during the Eastern Han dynasty. The blue color porcelain produced by Yue Kiln represented of its popular kind in the states of Han and Jin. A poem written during the Han dynasty told a story of the poet himself on a spring outing with his friends on a mountain for a tea party with his Yue Kiln tea sets.

In the Tang dynasty, the blue glazed porcelain in the south and the white glazed in north China gradually earned equal shares in the market. Lu Yu had a

White kettle with double gradin heads (Sui dynasty)

famous conclusion on that, "The tea soup (at that time) is slightly reddish, while the blue porcelain looks heavy in color with a touch of jade. When the two are matched together, they form a pleasing contrast in an elegant manner. Though Xingzhou porcelain shines in pure white and resembles silver, it won't be a good match for tea soup, for it's a bit too light in color." Lu Yu and others in the Tang dynasty considered blue glazed porcelain tea bowls as the best tea utensils.

This also helps us understand why the first choice of utensils for tea changed from blue porcelain to black one during the Song dynasty. The tea drinkers in those days usually whisked tea soups with a *chaxian* (the tea whisk) to form pure white foams. Black was undoubtedly the best choice in order to contrast with the white foams and more importantly, to help the judge decide which tea owner won. The five kilns—Ru, Guan, Ge, Jun and Ding— were known for the unprecedented beauty of their products. The fineness of the porcelain texture, the pureness of

Blue and white tea caddy covered with a lid (Jingdezhen Kiln, Ming dynasty)

The author's private collection: (Top) The 7501 ceramics specially produced for Chairman Mao Zedong has a shell as thin as that of an egg. (Bottom) Wenge porcelain tea tray

the glaze, the creation of the shape had reached a higher level. The crackle on the glaze surface from Ge Kiln winded like an earthworm. The pleasing flambé glaze color of Jun Kiln resembled pink clouds or roses. The tea cups made by Longquan Kiln (Celadon) were shaped like upside-down bamboo hats and covered completely in a light cyan glaze.

In the Ming dynasty, people's choices over the color of tea utensils enormously changed again. When loose tea came to their table, drinkers mainly used white, blue-white or colored porcelain from Jingdezhen Kiln. These cups accentuated the freshness of the green soup for they were regarded "as thin as paper, as white as jade, as sonorous as chime stone and as bright as mirror."

Blue and white tea cup (Jingdezhen Kiln, Ming dynasty)

Lu Jun glazed teapot (Yixing Kiln, Qing dynasty)

Porcelain during the Qing dynasty under the reigns of Emperors Kangxi, Yongzheng and Qianlong were the best of its kind throughout the country. New varieties such as famille rose and enamel porcelain came into existence. Innovations in its decoration included various inscriptions, legends, pictures of famous scenic sites and lucky patterns.

Porcelain tea utensils contain a gold mine of cultural messages from where we can breathe the lush scent of history. Someone can infer the time period in which it was fired from the picture and figures drawn on it. It would probably take an expert in collections and antiques to tell the age such a set belonged to.

Chinese tea drinkers have always emphasized the water used in tea ceremonies.

CHAPTER FOUR

TEA ART AND CEREMONIES

Tea has its periods and different styles as art, which can be roughly classified into three stages: the Boiled Tea, the Whipped Tea, and the Steeped Tea. The Chinese ethnic minority groups have also formed their own unique tea customs.

We moderns belong to the Steeped Tea stage. If using a main tea set, the two infusion manners are through the teapot or cups. Infusing by teapot means brewing the tea leaves inside the pot first, take the Qimen black tea, Pu'er or Da Hong Pao as an example, and then pour the liquor into cups. Obviously, infusing by cups means directly using the cup, glass or cover-bowl cup (*gaiwan*) to brew and drink. The latter is suitable for superior Spring tea such as Bi Luo Chun, Huangshan Maofeng, Junshan Yinzhen or Xihu Longjing tea picked before the Pure Brightness Festival.

How to appreciate the Chinese tea ceremonies?

It is very important to bear in mind that Chinese tea art has its unique aesthetic style. Its movements are like finger dancing with an opera-like plot. A graceful show of tea art is on when a tea sommelier slowly stretches out her wrists. While she fetches a tea utensil, you are seeing her fingers move like seeing the first blossom of a lotus flower. When she holds the cup and moves it, it's like an orchid floating in the air. While she pours the water, perhaps the kettle mouth is bobbing up and down like the nodding of a phoenix. While she turns the cup, its rim is displayed in full like a peacock spreading its tail. While she warms the cup, perhaps you are watching her fingers quickly roll the cup as if watching a traditional Chinese lion playing with a ball, or, while she pours out the last few drops of tea, it's like the general making his rounds, playing fair with every soldier of his troop without leaving anyone behind. The whole set of gestures are completed in a continuous gentle flow without any breaks, just like following the movements of Tai-Chi, where there seems to be a spirit floating and transferring in between, revealing the beauty and richness of its vitality.

Actually, a top master is a moving work of art during the tea ceremony. She gradually forms her own style that enriches her character, body language, and choreography to improve the performance. Next, you will see some pictures of the three main styles of Chinese tea art (photographs by Roy Le, staring Ling Yun). Normally the design of costumes, selection of tea sets and stage props as well as some unique processes of the tea ceremonies are presented according to the understanding and creativity of the tea master. So, you may also call the following ceremonies the "Ling Yun Style."

Longjing Tea Ceremony (using glass sets)

How to make a good cup of tea?

Let's take Longjing, the most famous Chinese tea, as an example. Personally I prefer *gaiwan*, but today's tea houses all use transparent glass. On the other hand, the glass is easy for us to watch the green leaves dance. Furthermore, the skill of using glass is relatively simple, allowing us to appreciate super-fine Longjing any place.

1. Make a bow.

2. Place the tools.

3. Appreciate the Longjing tea.

4. Appreciate the famous Hupao Spring water from Hangzhou City. Put a coin or other small flat things on it. If the coin can float, it shows the water, which has large surface tension, is suitable for making tea.

5. Warm the glass.

6. Put in tea.

Moisten.

Brew. Start with holding the kettle high to pour the water from above and then bring it closer to the glass… Repeat three times, like a phoenix nodding to express its appreciation to the guests.

7. Present the tea. The host must serve the tea respectfully using both hands to hold the glass, while saying softly "enjoy your tea". The guest, at the same time, should slightly move his body forward and express gratitude.

Enjoy drinking the tea.

Kung Fu Tea Art (using *Zisha* Tea Pot)

Kung Fu tea art originated in Chaozhou-Shantou District of Guangdong Province in South China, with Kung Fu actually meaning "brewing tea with great skill." It came into being in the Qing dynasty, and still retains the most ancient drinking methods, especially with tea sets and infusion technique. For instance, the four treasures of Kung Fu tea utensils include a special clay stove with matching kettle, the Yixing small teapot and thin white porcelain cups. On the other hand, we usually use Fenghuang Dancong from the Mount Phoenix region in Chaozhou or Wuyi rock tea alternative.

1. Beginning gesture: add water to the kettle.

2. Fan the stove.

3. Water the teapot and cups.

4. Place the tea on a clean white paper to arrange the leaves according to their sizes. Then move the tea leaves into the pot.

5. Lift the kettle high to brew.

6. Remove the foam. Put the lid back and pour the hot water over surface of the teapot.

7. Lion rolling the ball: clean the tea cups skillfully and gracefully in the boiling water.

8. Distribute the tea like the Lord Guan (Guan Yu, 160-219, general in the period of Three Kingdoms) making an inspection of the city wall.

9. Pour the tea until the last drop into every teacup

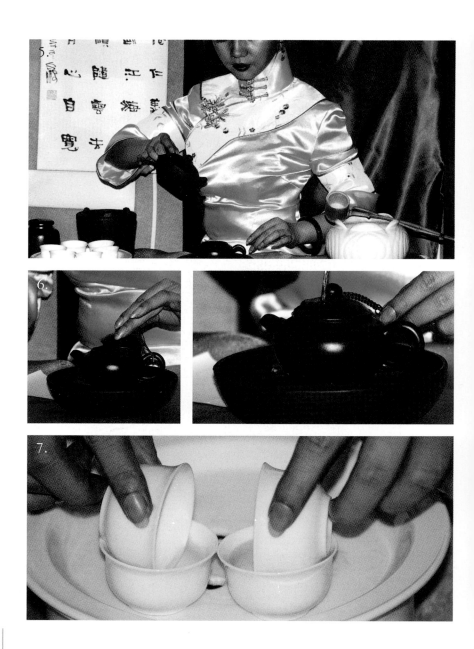

like the legendary General Han (Hai Xin, ?-196 BC, strategist in the Qin and Han dynasties) mustering the troops.

10. Presenting tea. When the host serves tea or adds water for his/her guests, some guests will knock the table rhythmically using bended middle finger and forefinger of their right hand to express their thanks.

Oriental Beauty's Tea Art (using porcelain sets)

Taiwan Oolong originated in Fujian and has formed its own characteristics. The Taiwanese also developed traditional tea art with their wisdom. Since we have watched an infusion with a small clay teapot, I will use porcelain *gaiwan* to carry on this demonstration.

1. Display the tea utensils.

2. Warm up the *gaiwan* and teacups.

3. Appreciate the tea.

4. Put in tea.

5. Initial soak.

6. Brew.

7. Move the foam.

8. Distribute the tea from the *gaiwan* with the thumb, index and middle fingers like three dragons escorting an ancient vessel.

9. Turn the cups upside down like a peacock spreading its tail to show its finest feathers.

10. Present the tea.

11. Enjoy the tea.

12. Sip the tea.

The theory of today's pressure deduction has its root in the Chinese Tao of tea.

CHAPTER FIVE

THE SPIRIT OF THE CHINESE TAO OF TEA

Tea is the carrier of the Chinese culture, where the values and ideal Tao of the Chinese can be found.

Tao, the most supreme conception of the Chinese philosophies, signifies universal law, ultimate truth, and the general rule governing all motions, or the essence or origin of everything on earth. Mainstream of the Chinese culture used to be the "complementation of Confucianism and Taoism." After the Sui and Tang dynasties, the general trend moved to the "trinity of Confucianism, Zennism and Taoism." Therefore, for Tao, there is the Tao of Confucianism, the Tao of Taoism, and the Tao of Buddhism. None of them are necessarily the same. I heard the Song allegory of the "Three Vinegar Tasters" to explain the development of the three doctrines. Sakyamuni, Confucius, and Laozi (Lao-tzu) once stood before a jar of vinegar—the emblem of life—and each dipped in his finger to taste the brew. The Confucius found the vinegar sour, the Buddha called it bitter, and Laozi pronounced it sweet.

The Chinese Tao of Tea, the philosophy of tea, is also a trinity. The art of tea-drinking aims to cultivate Tao, which comprises the three key fields of tea etiquette, art and Zen. First, tea etiquette refers to the rituals and rules in tea activities. Second, tea art refers to the workmanship with the tea including preparing tea utensils, choosing water, controlling the heat, timing the cooking, and serving the tea. Lastly, tea Zen means to develop temperament, comprehend the truth of Tao and maintain fitness.

Someone has missed the real charm of tea if he takes a careful sip and utters with disappointment, "Oh! It's bitter." He has only experienced its taste without touching the inner spirit of the Chinese Tao of Tea. During its thousands of years' long history, tea has been gradually endowed with a unique cultural value and aesthetic philosophy. Tea signifies politics, culture, economics and even Zen as you'll see in the following philosophies.

Confucianism

The core of Confucianism is etiquette and harmony. For example, the Chinese have the custom "When a guest arrives, a cup of tea will be served." After seating the guest, the host will serve tea as a way to welcome him. During the conversation, tea will add to the friendly atmosphere. At the end of the visit, the host raises the tea cup as a way to say it's time for "goodbye."

Another example of Confucianism's philosophy occurs when you enjoy tea at

Confucius used to be a band conductor. His favorite instrument was the *guqin*, called "the king of Chinese musical instruments". Playing *guqin* and drinking tea is to reach the harmony of body and soul in tranquility. In 2003, UNESCO awarded the art of *guqin* the title "Masterpiece of the Oral and Intangible Heritage of Humanity."

one of today's tea houses in China. You'll find all tea cups only 70% full instead of completely full. The tea house owner or the tea servers will explain to you that this means "Seventy percent tea and thirty percent affection." You may have the same question as me, why not thirty percent tea and seventy percent affection? Why not show more affection? In fact, the "thirty percent affection" explanation is a modern misinterpretation of a tradition that originated from the Han and Tang dynasties. The remaining space in the tea cup means to keep one's mind open, implying the moral of "Pride hurts and modesty benefits." I have heard a story derived from this venerable Chinese philosophy. A respectable Taoist priest received a college professor who came to acquire Tao. After chatting for a few minutes, the priest stood up to serve tea for the guest. The priest filled up the cup, but continued pouring in more tea. "It's full! No tea can be filled in anymore!" cried the professor, who was staring at his cup of overflowing tea. The priest answered, "You are just like the cup of tea, fulfilled by your own judgments, ideas and assumptions in your brain. If the cup is not emptied, how can I reveal the truth of Tao to you?"

Taoism

Tea also contains the wisdom and aesthetics of the Chinese Taoism. Laozi, named Li Er, was the founder of Taoism. Confucius once returned from a visit with Laozi in Luoyang City and praised him as unfathomable like a dragon flying in clouds, meaning that Laozi was the wisest. Taoism is a way of life which emphasizes the self, accepts the secular, and harmonizes one with the rest of the world. Together with Confucianism, Taoism has become one of the major pillars of the Chinese culture as well.

The "thirty percent affection"

The calligraphy on tea drinking of the Ming dynasty

Painting of *Laozi Riding an Ox*

Similar to Tai-Chi Quan (shadow boxing), also created by the Taoists, Taoism maintains that the art of tea rests with empty quietness, a natural way of doing, and a combination of motion and stillness in the nurturing of a noble spirit.

Zennism

Reading the history of tea, you will see its close relationship to Buddhism from coming across numerous temples and many accomplished monks. The boom of tea drinking in the Tang dynasty was indeed a result of the rise of Buddhism, especially Zennism. When learning Zen, one should meditate with the eyes closed. Tea developed into necessity because it was easy to fall asleep with this posture. Subsequently, it soon became fashionable

The monks gathered before the figure of Dharma and drank tea from a single bowl with the profound formality of a holy sacrament in Chinese Zen Buddhism. This Zen ritual developed into the tea ceremony of Japan in the fifteenth century.

to drink tea in various temples with all the monks joining in to plant, collect and process tea leaves. Famous teas are often made from celebrated temples.

In the world of the Chinese Tao of Tea float the ripples of Zenist philosophy. These philosophies are unwritten, passed on by the soul, and grasped by the self in an instant.

CHAPTER SIX

THE HEALTH BENEFITS

More than a widely-consumed beverage in the world, tea is a friend for Zen meditation that helps us gain inner peace. Besides, fine teas, hot or over ice, are strongly recommended because of their positive health benefits. A medical book from the Tang dynasty over one thousand years ago said, "Tea cures every disease." It may sound a little bit exaggerated. The Chinese, however, have been using tea for thousands of years for its different effects such as weight loss, lowering blood pressure, the prevention of cancers and curing stress-related diseases.

Modern science illustrates that tea has a very low fat and caloric content as well as containing plenty of protein and vitamins. Tea leaves are a rich natural source of polyphenolic antioxidant catechins (often incorrectly referred to as tannins), aromatic or essential oils and caffeine. The polyphenol is the most important element because it provides the greatest positive health benefit through a quite complex mechanism.

Kills Bacteria

Tea's medicinal properties are not a new discovery. According to various ancient Chinese medical books, tea liquid can cure hepatitis, dysentery as well as enteritis. Today, there is still a tradition in China where brewed tea leaves are placed on small wounds, inflamed gums or red swollen eyes to speed recovery. All kinds of teas, especially green tea, black tea and Oolong, have been linked to the control of diarrhea and inhibiting unhealthy bacterial cell growth such as Salmonella, while promoting healthy stomach bacterial growth.

Aids Digestion

After tea became nationally fashionable during the Tang dynasty, tea drinking was accordingly introduced to ethnic minorities and foreign countries as the essence of a civilized way of living. While learning The Chinese Tao of Tea, the Koryo State, a neighboring country of China, explained in their records why tea was tremendously popular: "People of the Tang Empire all ate meat. Whereas tea

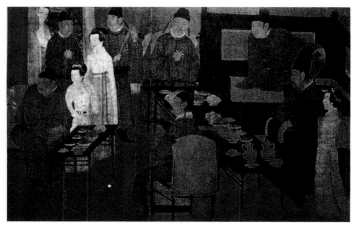

Tea served during the ancient Chinese banquet

served as a way to improve digestion and in turn, eliminate jaundice (a traditional Chinese medical term, which referred to the discomforts brought on by eating plenty of meats). In areas of Tibet, Xinjiang and Mongolia where inhabitants eat beef, mutton, butter and cheese as their staple foods, there is a saying 'Can't live without tea, even for a day'."

Tea always refreshes yourself.

Fights Aging

Several medical research studies show that green tea leaves contain a very powerful antioxidant called polyphenolic catechins, which can lower the amount of DNA damaging free radicals in the body. Catechin, which is not found in coffee, has an anti-oxidation function 40 to 100 times stronger than vitamin C. Not all teas contain the same amount of catechins. Non-fermented green teas such as Longjing retain many more catechins than semi-fermented teas such as Oolong. The fully fermented black teas have the least amount of catechins. Furthermore, polyphenolic catechins may reduce the risk of age-related degenerative brain disorders such as Alzheimer disease. These elements are effective for anti-aging.

Assists Weight Loss

Tea helps the body lose weight by burning more calories, according to the studies from *The American Journal of Clinical Nutrition* in 1999. A study of the impact of

Pu'er tea, which can help someone stay slim, can be divided into "raw" (top) and "crusted" (bottom) types. Fresh made Pu'er tea called "raw" is often wild and untamable in its herbal nature. Once it turns into older crusted tea, it becomes gentler for the stomach. So the latter is more suitable for those new to drinking Pu'er.

water, green tea and Oolong on the Basal Metabolic Rate (BMR), a rate the body metabolizes energy, found tea could affect the BMR. Water has no particular function on BMR. Green tea can raise 4 calories of the BMR per hour, while Oolong can raise it by 9 calories. The function of this can last up to five hours. In other words, only one cup of 300cc Oolong tea can burn 40 calories. This is equivalent to fast walking for 15 minutes or climbing stairs for 10 minutes.

Pu'er tea, which can help someone stay slim, can be divided into "raw" and "crusted" types. Fresh made Pu'er tea called "raw" is often wild and untamable in its herbal nature. Once it turns into older crusted tea, it becomes gentler for the stomach. So the latter is more suitable for those new to drinking Pu'er.

Prevents Cancer

Another study was designed to investigate the effects of two main constituents of green tea, EGCG (Epi-Gallo-Catechin-Gallate) and caffeine, on intestinal tumor-igenesis in Apcmin/+ mice, a recognized mouse model for human intestinal cancer, and to elucidate possible mechanisms involved in the inhibitory action of the active constituent (Cancer Res. Vol.65 pp. 10623-10631 & Biol. Pharm. Bull. Vol.30 pp. 200-204). Also, research conducted in 1998 suggested that men who drank three cups of green tea a day were 30 percent less likely to develop prostrate cancer.

Lowers Blood Pressure & Protects the Heart

The antioxidant substances, flavonoid and EGCG

in tea, may delay the development of hypertension and reduce blood pressure. In a population study with Norwegian men and women, higher intake of black tea was linked to a lower systolic blood pressure in the cohort. In a study on men and women above age 20, in comparison to those who did not drink tea, the risk of hypertension went down 46 percent in those who drank 2-3 cups of tea per day, and 65 percent in those drinking more than 3 cups per day. Another study showed the same favourable effects of tea consumption on systolic and diastolic blood pressure in older women.

The health effect of EGCG helps to lower the bad cholesterol (LDL) by an average of 10 percent and improved the ratio between LDL and the good cholesterol (HDL). Where dangerous cholesterol has already stuck to the artery, flavornoid helps to prevent it from damaging the inner lining. Tea protects against heart disease by preventing the hypertrophy of one's heart, which can stop blood from forming abnormal clots that could cause heart attacks and strokes (Drug Metab. Dispos. Vol.16 pp.98-103). The process of this mechanism is like water flowing more smoothly after the build-up has been removed from old pipes.

Treats Colds and Flu

Asian people have long used white tea to eliminate

Tea helps your body lose weight by burning more calories, according to the studies.

fever in children who exhibit symptoms of cold and flu viruses. You can also simply drink green tea because its EGCG can cause the inhibition of the hemagglutinin and the neuraminidase, the two transmission tools of flu (Antiviral Res. Vol.68 pp66-74). I drink tea a few times daily in the early spring and winter to boost my immunity, adding a slice of lemon in a cup of black tea with a ½ teaspoon of mint. If you are sick, you will notice a gradual decrease of your influenza by drinking tea. A drop of honey in a cup of black tea also eases a sore throat. This therapy is better than drinking warm water mixed with salt.

Protects from the Harm of Electromagnetic Radiation

Protection from radiation is a unique effect of tea. In modern times, electromagnetic radiation is everywhere. In the office, there are computers, photocopiers, laser printers and fax machines. At all times, cell phones are always near by whether you're using yours or someone is using one right next to you. Back at home, there are still microwaves, ovens as well as televisions. Both epicatechin and vitamins are present in significant quantities in green tea. It is known that these compounds are able to inhibit the oxidation of radiation harm. For couch potatoes, take a cup of tea while watching TV.

Refreshes Yourself

Caffeine may not be so bad. When the legendary Shen Nong and Bodhi-Dharma tasted tea, each was exhilarated to find that it cleared their minds. The amount of caffeine in green tea (about 20mg/150ml) is much less than coffee (about 100mg/150ml). Drinking a cup of green tea is helpful in your recovery after working overnight.

Other Health Benefits

In addition to the above effects, the consumption of tea has been shown to have many other health benefits.

Tea protects you from the harm of electromagnetic radiation as its unique effect in modern times.

These include:

Tooth care: Tea can reduce the amount of plaque on the teeth by killing the bacteria that forms it. Galconoid in tea also helps to fight cavities by stopping bacteria from sticking to the teeth. The traditional Chinese would clean their mouths and teeth by gargling with tea after getting up every morning.

Builds the bone: Falconoid, found in tea protects the bones.

Diabetes: Tea is able to influence the body's sensitivity to insulin and affects glucose tolerance levels.

Fights UV light: Catechin plays a role in the prevention of skin cancers and is thought to be able to protect the skin from ultra violet radiation.

Anything to Avoid?

Due to its caffeine content, tea should be avoided by infants, young children and those who have lost sleep.

Tea-drinking is like a spa or yoga for your body and soul at anytime, anywhere.

Pregnant and breastfeeding women should drink tea in limited amounts.

For individuals who feel nauseated while drinking tea without milk, it's best to eat something small such as half of a biscuit. For people required to follow a caffeine free diet, the quantities of caffeine in both green and black (about 55mg/150ml) teas are significant. Those with a stomach-ache should drink tea after meals.

Bibliography

1. Laozi (Lao-tzu), *Dao De Jing (Tao Te Ching)*, Shanxi Guji Press, 2000

2. Kongzi (Confucius), *Analects of Confucius (Lun Yu)*, Shanxi Guji Press, 1999

3. Lu Yu, *The Classic of Tea*, Zhejiang Guji Press, 2004

4. Wu Juenong, *Review to The Classic of Tea*, China Agriculture Press, 2005

5. Kakuzo Okakura, *The Book of Tea*, Charles E. Tuttle,1998

6. Ma Weidu, *Classical Chinese Doors & Windows*, China Architecture Industry Press, 2006

Dynasties in Chinese History

Xia Dynasty	2070 BC – 1600 BC
Shang Dynasty	1600 BC – 1046 BC
Zhou Dynasty	1046 BC – 256 BC
Western Zhou Dynasty	1046 BC – 771 BC
Eastern Zhou Dynasty	770 BC – 256 BC
Spring and Autumn Period	770 BC – 476 BC
Warring States Period	475 BC – 221 BC
Qin Dynasty	221 BC – 206 BC
Han Dynasty	206 BC – 220 AD
Western Han Dynasty	206 BC – 25 AD
Eastern Han Dynasty	25 AD – 220 AD
Three Kingdoms	220 AD – 280 AD
Wei	220 AD – 265 AD
Shu Han	221 AD – 263 AD
Wu	222 AD – 280 AD
Jin Dynasty	265AD – 420AD
Western Jin Dynasty	265 AD – 316 AD
Eastern Jin Dynasty	317 AD – 420 AD
Northern and Southern Dynasties	420 AD – 589 AD
Southern Dynasties	420 AD – 589 AD
Northern Dynasties	439 AD – 581 AD
Sui Dynasty	581 AD – 618 AD
Tang Dynasty	618 AD – 907 AD
Five Dynasties and Ten States	907 AD – 960 AD
Five Dynasties	907 AD – 960 AD
Ten States	902 AD – 979 AD
Song Dynasty	960 AD – 1279
Northern Song Dynasty	960 AD – 1127
Southern Song Dynasty	1127 – 1279
Liao Dynasty	916 AD – 1125
Jin Dynasty	1115 – 1234
Xixia Dynasty	1038 – 1227
Yuan Dynasty	1279 – 1368
Ming Dynasty	1368 – 1644
Qing Dynasty	1644 – 1911